WATER AND AIR

S.E. McKenzie

S. E. MCKENZIE

WATER AND AIR

DEDICATION
To everyone who has been left out in the cold.

S. E. MCKENZIE

This book is a book of speculative fiction.
Characters, companies, governments, places, events, are
either products of the author's imagination or used
fictitiously. Any resemblance to persons (living or
dead), companies, governments, places and/or events, is
a coincidence.

WATER AND AIR

TABLE OF CONTENTS

S. E. MCKENZIE

WATER AND AIR

I

OH how it feasts
On innocence
Blank slate so misunderstood

Free from a guilty mind
Still pure and kind
Where intent and content

Invisible
Divisible
Never sustainable

You cannot ignore its roar
As it comes crashing down
Harder than ever before.

It cannot be policed

For it is the Microbeast;
It must climb the hill
And hunt prey to kill;

WATER AND AIR

Food chain
Gets yanked
One more time again

OH how it feasts
On innocence
Blank slate so misunderstood

Free from a guilty mind
Still pure and kind
Where intent and content

Mutual beneficiality
Made this city
A long time ago.

That was the time
Of less crime
And exploitation

When everyone had a chance to live;
Until the arrival
Of the Microbeast.

S. E. MCKENZIE

Social power
Micro aggression
Macro suppression

What was once free
Is now in a cage.
What was once free

Burns in rage.
Must live his days like he is going to die.
Ignored intent and content; just a lie.

Touching him; half dead and half alive;
The victims of the Microbeast try to survive.
They hide every day

From their dictator;
They try hard to not become a hater;
Never too willing to give love a try.

OH how it feasts
On innocence
Blank slate so misunderstood

Free from a guilty mind
Still pure and kind
Where intent and content

WATER AND AIR

Is so aware
How hard it is to care
Too late to cry

Living everyday ready to die
Even though there are still
New things to try.

Too young to feel so old
Too young to feel so cold
The Microbeast has its hold.

II
The big guns

Are standing by
Some are flying in the sky.

Negativity all around
Hate burning
In the ground

Never acknowledging why.

You can hear it roaring;
You can't block the sound;
For the Microbeast

S. E. MCKENZIE

Is said not to be just controlled
By agglomerates gone by;
It is controlled by its appetite

Which can never die.
Will fight until the end
For the right to rule and fool

Using fear to control and rule.

Through micro aggressors
And macro oppressors
Who need no vote;

So civilized they say
To bulldoze shacks
Of the have nots

"We do it to beautify"
They say
Those people will die anyway.

OH how it feasts
On innocence
Blank slate so misunderstood

WATER AND AIR

Free from a guilty mind
Still pure and kind
Where intent and content

Built this city, a long time ago.

So civilized they say
To overkill
The underfed

We will make them go away
They don't belong here anyway
They were not born or bred here.

III
Ruling by fear
Took its toll
For the Microbeast was always near.

Mary phoned the cops on Sam
She accused him of being a troll;
She needed a man in a different role.

The canine unit chased Sam down the street
The dog treated Sam's arm
Like a piece of meat.

S. E. MCKENZIE

And the Microbeast said
All power is in the head
So cover your ego don't let it show

So you will still have one tomorrow.
For no one cared
And no one dared

For the destruction fed the Microbeast;

It was such a feast.
Sam's arm could not be repaired
And his heart grew cold

Sam still loved Mary
And became a merchant of gold
Until he grew old.

What happened next
Was never told.
Their house and things are now sold.

Some say they went overseas
So they could begin again
Free from memories and yesterday's pain.

WATER AND AIR

IV

There was an image

That was held up to the sky
No substance or life did it have

And no real person need apply
For the Microbeast
Would rather be alone

As it enjoyed its feast.
It was more true than true
And more real than real

The Microbeast
Could manipulate
How many would feel

Lost in hate.

They feel distain
Without refrain;
They beg the Microbeast to detain

Him; for evermore;
Ignored intent and content;
Inhuman Microbeast will now reign,

S. E. MCKENZIE

As tear drops fell gently from the heavens above.

V

For one; it was Laissez-faire;
And regulated for another;
Rivals could never be equals.

How could they be?
Don't you see?
That is how the Microbeast paves its way.

The Microbeast was in the heart.
The Microbeast was in the ground.
The Microbeast was everywhere;

While Jack and Jill climbed the hill
To get a pail of water;
As it rained the ground turned into mud all around.

Mud went into the water
And smoke went into the air;
Out of sight; Laissez-faire.

The water could not speak;
And the air could not scream;
Jack and Jill awoke from the dream

WATER AND AIR

And felt so weak.

VI
Deeds done in the past

Will linger on
No one to blame, they had all gone.

Without water or air
The most powerful
Of all could only crawl.

Trees were cut down all around
A long time ago.
Now mud will sometimes flow

Into the rivers and streams.
There were a few cries of protest
And they were soon put under arrest.

We must stay Laissez-faire.
The politicians said before the voting few
You know who.

We are depending on you
To ignore
Those with less.

S. E. MCKENZIE

OH how it feasts
On innocence
Blank slate so misunderstood

Free from a guilty mind
Still pure and kind
Where intent and content

Must stand strong
When the heart has been broken
And the pain has awoken.

So close your eyes
To inequality
Because that is the way it must be.

So you can have more;
There is no equality
Amongst rivals

Just like war;

And without earth, air and water
There can't be survival
Even for the fittest

WATER AND AIR

As Jack and Jill climbed the hill
They tried not to fall
It was a long way to go for water

And they did not want to lose a drop
They had to water their crop
And they were working against the clock

For without water
Life as they knew it
Would come to a stop

Together they carried the pail
For without water
What was once strong would grow frail.

VII
Life is all around

In water and air.
It is just the beginning

Nothing much to do; Laissez-faire
Until you run out
Then you will scream and shout

S. E. MCKENZIE

As panic sets in
Many surrendered
They were too weak to fight.

For they were withering away
Some called it genocide
Others lied

And joined the other side
For freedom meant nothing
Without water or air.

Vulnerability
Fear of another
Oppression

Abuse of power
Over another
Hypocrisy

An act of war

WATER AND AIR

VIII
A miracle of Nature undone
Around water, air and sun
Sacred combination

Of Nature and Nurture
Renewal in gentle sleep
To be deprived of Nature

Nature will take and give back
Yes, Nature will take over
That is Nature's way

Nature can force us to take a nap
Where ever we may be
Soon we will sleep in Eternity.

Jill stood at the mouth of the river
As the wind blew
She stood with babe in arms

No one knew
How she fell into the raging river
That fateful day

The Force of Nature was moving too fast
Rational Life Force
In action

Does it need to be controlled
To be sold
To the highest bidder?

Now Jack was half the man
He used to be
And his loss would haunt him

For Eternity,
He would never be free
From wondering what could have been.

IX

The water felt colder than air
Protected by civilization
It was a climate of Laissez-faire.

In another forgotten city
That time flew by
Too fast to understand and no longer pretty.

Jack paced back and forth
Lost in his sorrow
He feared the emptiness of tomorrow

WATER AND AIR

Living in a forgotten city
Mud sometimes fell into the lake
An act of fate, result of an ancient mistake

Controlled by ghosts
From an era gone by
Jack tried to start his life

All over again

X

Jack could see Jill through shadows
Descending from Eternity;
He wanted to get closer

So he climbed the tree;
For it could reach the heavens above;
Jack could not let go of his love.

As Jack climbed into the sky
He found a world
Much bigger than he

Where piles of gold
Were here and there
In another world of laissez-faire

Beside the piles of gold
There was a man who was very old
And he was a giant of a man

S. E. MCKENZIE

His name was Sam

As Jack couldn't help but stare
Sam fell asleep in his chair
Sam snored so loud

It gave Jack a scare
But the Microbeast said
Think of the feast instead

Jack hurried down the tree
And left Sam's land
With a bag of gold in hand

As he climbed the hill
He thought of Jill
And cursed the river's chill

Jack felt Jill's aura faintly
Strong presence
Felt saintly

Who can I grow to be
Without my true love by my side?
Will this gold free me from all this pain inside?

WATER AND AIR

XI

There wasn't a day
That went by
That Jack didn't think of Jill

And the pain never went away

The pail of water
Turned to rust
And in humanity Jack had lost his trust

The gold was good to him though
It gave him a new perspective on life
Because he now had running water

He had no reason to climb the hill
No reason at all
But he did anyway

Just to see Jill's shadow
Descending from Eternity
Reminding Jack that he had a long way to go

Before he could join Jill
Above the hill
Some still called heaven.

XII

OH how it feasts
On innocence
Blank slate so misunderstood

Free from a guilty mind
Still pure and kind
Where intent and content

Were not held under suspicion
Debt bondage
Next form of slavery

Without a plan
And little hope
How would the pre-living cope?

Would they look into the sky
And wonder why
An age so draconian

Could never die

WATER AND AIR

It was easy to convince
The lost generation
To tie the unborn

To debt from before
Like water and air
It was all Laissez-faire

OH how it feasts
On innocence
Blank slate so misunderstood

Free from a guilty mind
Still pure and kind
Where intent and content

Never ceased to wonder
As the Microbeast's roar
Could never be ignored

For it set the pace
And shaped the human race
Without needing a face

XIII
The Microbeast
Will feast tonight
Under candlelight

Jack wondered why
He must jump over the candlestick
For it was quite cruel

If one thought about the words
Though no one ever did
For it was forbidden

To think
Jack would rather feast
With the Microbeast

And forget
His pain and sorrow
For a while.

THE END

WATER AND AIR

WATER AND AIR
Produced by S.E. McKenzie Productions
First PRINT Edition January 2015

ISBN: 978-1-928069-32-4
Copyright © 2015 by S. E. McKenzie

S. E. MCKENZIE

Enquiries: 1(778)992-2453
Mailing Address:
S. E. McKenzie Productions
168 B 5th St.
Courtenay, BC
V9N 1J4

Email Address:
messidartha@aol.com

Check Out Sarah McKenzie's Amazon Page:
http://www.amazon.com/Sarah-
McKenzie/e/B00H9RWX48/ref=ntt_dp_epwbk_0

www.ingramcontent.com/pod-product-compliance
Lightning Source LLC
Chambersburg PA
CBHW060951050426
42337CB00054B/4507